IN THREE LINES

ReBalancing

By

Charley Elbow

IN THREE LINES

ReBalancing

ReBalancing

Longing to belong
   What they never realised
      You're born you belong

A tadpole decides
   Their chosen mini climate
      Determines their growth

My voice was stolen
   Years of silence and grief then
      This new voice was born

ReBalancing

They seem separate
    Solitary seasoned trees
        Yet roots intertwine

Earth sings as she spins
    Daytime moon reassuring
        Faith in the unseen

Clock's run out of tocks
    Lots of ticks right wrong or not
        Just the tocks got lost

ReBalancing

In the darkest times
    Hope is twitchily dozing
       Eager to awake

Some walls can't be breached
    But love kindness and patience
       Might help build a door

Though now an adult
    Nan's cakes are the best presents
       Love in every crumb

ReBalancing

Grieving moon and stars
    Cradle the Earth in their arms
        Forlorn injured child

Deep down in a hole
    Ladder appears friendly shout
        I know the way out

Be the difference
    Bear witness for other folk
        Acknowledge their lives

ReBalancing

Today is the day
For smashing the pigeonholes
We find ourselves in

A box marked later
Neatly folded ambitions
Quietly unfurl

I relate to sloths
Determined inquisitive
Strengths other than speed

ReBalancing

Misleadings mistakes
    Missteps misdeeds misgivings
        Don't miss escape routes

Condensing problems
    To seventeen syllables
        Haiku therapy

I found myself lost
    Left right here beside myself
        Upside down side up

ReBalancing

Spying loneliness
 Weather's breath rustles their hair
  Scarred hearts breathe again

Stitching rich magic
 Into the fabric of life
  She smiles satisfied

Wit wisdom whimsy
 Unbound by reality
  Stories set us free

ReBalancing

Hidden forgotten
Cobbles glow from spilt sunshine
Truly paved in gold

Don't blink tears away
Lift your head and look through them
Salty sweet prisms

Stage lit by fireflies
Pine needles pirouetting
Teasing gravity

ReBalancing

Riddles puzzles quotes
    How many are red herrings
        Which ones need we solve

Stealthily we can
    Build a portfolio of
        Little rebellions

Two tiny gremlins
    Lodged in each side of my brain
        Vie for attention

ReBalancing

Swift Nature upgrade
Their shed is now a castle
Because of its moat

Colourless outlook
Our brains can redecorate
Repaint our landscapes

Bees begin to hum
Dandelions keep the time
Bluebells chime the tune

ReBalancing

Friendships can be forged
      In love laughter and distress
            Invisible links

When things go badly
      I've learnt to remind myself
            No grit means no pearls

Cares tiptoe away
      Tension takes a mini break
            Loose limbed relaxing

ReBalancing

Some pages missing
A few stories rewritten
My mind's library

Anywhere is home
Any shape size space moment
All it needs is love

Sleep imprisons dreams
Fantastical happenings
Unbidden untrue

ReBalancing

Hunched bedraggled mouse
Too soggy for scampering
No cute umbrella

Battles for sound space
Harsh staccato rhetoric
Peacefulness echoes

Squirrels chat leaves laugh
Newly hatched cloudlets scamper
Sunshine feeds my veins

ReBalancing

Striding into rain
Man and long leggéd lurcher
Matching red raincoats

Many an hour spent
Fretting about the future
Now gets forgotten

Skinned knees hugging trees
Playing conkers hide and seek
Home made scones and jam

ReBalancing

Caught in every cell
    Air breathed sights seen glory held
      Felled oak merely sleep

Washed up on sleep's shore
    Interrupted incomplete
      Detritus of dreams

Grudgingly trudging
    Hauling its chilly backpack
      Winter fades again

ReBalancing

Misery sidles
  Silently up next to joy
    Keen for company

Revived by slumber
  Shrugging off mossy jackets
    Gleeful ferns unfurl

Ironically
  What we all have plenty of
    Is our uniqueness

ReBalancing

Hidden in tree tops
Avian soap operas
Warbled in the wind

Unsealing our fates
Can be painful heartbreaking
And liberating

I resent winter
It steals my light but does leave
Brief dazzles of white

ReBalancing

On nights such as these
 Spirits swing on crescent moons
 Starshine fills the air

High tides exciting
 Low tides strangely alluring
 More secrets exposed

Stress saturated
 Change habits patterns break moulds
 Do not break yourself

ReBalancing

Banter and teasing
Insults wrapped up as humour
Unwrap reject leave

To make it happen
Believe that part that believes
One hundred per cent

Alone not lonely
Both exhausted and content
Shy not retiring

ReBalancing

Leaves hurled at windows
    Skies spit and weep with fury
      Autumnal tantrums

Old Nursery Rhymes
    Considered signs of their times
      What would today's say

Blend into the crowd
    When it suits your purposes
      Useful camouflage

ReBalancing

We tend to focus
On the middle of pictures
Contemplate edges

Glossy blackbird preens
Ruffles puffs shimmies and struts
Confidence boosted

In all my Julys
I never thought to wonder
What colour is hope

ReBalancing

Beginnings and ends
Loops spirals infinity
Ends and beginnings

Slightly misaligned
Not quite fitting imperfect
Proudly eccentric

In difficult times
Try stepping outside yourself
Offer good advice

ReBalancing

Magic carpet rides
>*Huge vertiginous vistas*
>>*All viewed from my bed*

The day's looking worn
>*Like heels of favourite shoes*
>>*Well lived in enjoyed*

Rescued penguin chick
>*Hovers unsure at the shore*
>>*Dawdles then trots home*

ReBalancing

As one door closes
     Depending on force of course
          It slams or doesn't

Heather honour guard
     Stand sturdily protecting
          Budding ingénue

Frenzies of envy
     Unsocial media storm
          Frictional fiction

ReBalancing

So regimented
> *Please settle a while while I*
> *Order the chaos*

The moment you're born
> *You shaped space is created*
> *Time never forgets*

Nondescript puddle
> *Collector of shiny things*
> *Exhibits at night*

ReBalancing

Castles made from sand
Crafted by a small child's hand
Cherished by the sea

Night berates itself
For overstaying welcomes
It resolves more care

A muddle of chores
Clamouring insistently
Pour coffee ponder

ReBalancing

Resisting this flow
    Smooths and softens sharp edges
        Stepping stones lead home

Say relax I tense
    Say let it all out I clench
        Say must my heels twitch

Stair pixie confused
    By where on the stairs to be
        Here there everywhere

ReBalancing

Some days lay heavy
     Small actions take huge effort
          Each one a triumph

Tumultuous times
     Metaphorical blinds drawn
          Cosy calm inside

Atop rustic gates
     Perch agéd squirrels swapping
          Nuggets of wisdom

ReBalancing

Sun dwells on the edge
  Reluctant to lose her view
    Because it's of you

My body ages
  My head has happily stayed
    Somewhere near nineteen

Floors can be ceilings
  Ceilings can also be floors
    Doors do not need walls

ReBalancing

Ignoring the noise
Along with years comes freedoms
Caution downgraded

Always on the march
Trailing behind in their wake
I ride precious waves

We're wisps on the wind
Ultimately comforting
Whispers are still heard

ReBalancing

Holding my breath yet
    Dust motes twirl in sweet sunlight
        Then instantly stop

It's worth potting them
    Seeds of your great ideas
        Feed them see what grows

Windows everywhere
    Lights on lights off curtains closed
        So many stories

ReBalancing

Etched by the ocean
 Fleetingly shared swept away
 Aeons of wisdom

Up the chimney flue
 Broken conversations float
 Waiting for Santa

Bad decisions made
 We know that we can't rewind
 But we can reboot

ReBalancing

Braving the silence
Beneath the pulse and blood rush
Poetry resides

First I acknowledge
My guilt grief fear worries woe
Accept then release

Golden wood nymphs dance
Foxtrotting 'cross autumn leaves
Rustling ovation

ReBalancing

I'm planning a coup
*   To overthrow dark winters*
*   Extend summer's reign*

Assumptions pollute
*   How about starting afresh*
*   Hi pleased to meet you*

Pointed triangles
*   Parallels never can meet*
*   Circles seem complete*

ReBalancing

A gap in the clouds
 Stars dazzle my heart once more
  Ancient love affair

Splattering of rain
 Suddenly intrudes upon
  Water lily peace

Foundations shaken
 With the right care and patience
  Safer ground restored

ReBalancing

My creative mind
    Crushed for years by teacher's words
      Recently whispered

January blues
    Those moments after sunset
      Day melds into night

Inhabit your skin
    Unapologetic'ly
      Look life in the eye

ReBalancing

Restless for progress
      To grow taller older wise
            Some measured progress

I'm grown up so why
      Do family gatherings
            Scare my inner child

Feeling frozen they
      Recall cherished memories
            Relive them and glow

ReBalancing

Retuning my ears
To block negativity
Password protected

Ponderous river
Slowed by reminiscences
From the dawn of time

Inner traffic lights
Frequently jammed on the red
More go is needed

ReBalancing

Hope strides through the room
Dislodging cobwebs of gloom
Despondency melts

Silver edged evenings
As hush caresses the land
I hear comets sing

We were taught to speak
Read write run hide but rarely
Taught how to just be

ReBalancing

See beneath the skin
　　Bodies are but containers
　　　　Magic's worth finding

At each tether's end
　　Another can be tethered
　　　　Ad infinitum

Cultivate kindness
　　Nothing special is required
　　　　It grows where it lands

ReBalancing

Autumn shuffles in
Hoping no-one will notice
One breath at a time

A tiny tickle
In the outskirts of my mind
Itching for freedom

Despite what is said
Our tears are never wasted
Angels bathe in them

ReBalancing

Barrier strewn path
Judgement assumption and fear
Learning to hurdle

Open the floodgates
Drench yourself in great daydreams
Return replenished

They assumed wisdom
Came with ageing like wrinkles
Patiently perplexed

ReBalancing

Above the hubbub
Below the roar of starbirth
Golden eagles soar

Wildly sleep deprived
However hard they may try
Dots will not be joined

Leaning round the bends
Mainly going with the flow
Cheeky trips off piste

ReBalancing

Unforeseen buffet
Tasting all the day's flavours
Need time to digest

Witness has been borne
Raw power of gentleness
In the eye of storms

Above and below
The curvature of the Earth
Infinite wonder

ReBalancing

Reinvent yourself
    Discarding your least best parts
      Enhancing the rest

The shifting of sands
    Can both destruct and construct
      Fluidly designed

Child's scars of mistrust
    Vanishing into the past
      Love patiently healed

ReBalancing

Once autumn has struck
*   With breezes billows and gusts*
*   Mischief surrounds us*

Friends are tricky things
*   Right person right time magic*
*   Wrong one illusion*

Storing them all up
*   All my well earned Brownie points*
*   Just in case I slip*

ReBalancing

Creaking with the weight
Trees laden with snow worries
Know the thaw will come

Owls yearning lament
Stirs something deep in our souls
Otherwise unreached

Trying to make sense
Find explanations meaning
We're not always told

ReBalancing

Moonlit midnight sprites
Going about their business
Ride on shooting stars

However far through
The novel of your own life
Choose the next plot twist

Hassled and harried
No zig zagging to the nest
Direct flights only

ReBalancing

Neat exterior
  Whirlwinds of inner turmoil
    Balance will be reached

Struggling to weigh up
  Pros and cons encompassing
    Imponderables

Definitely a
  Wrap ourselves up stay indoors
    Warm cosy doze day

ReBalancing

Glaringly loud sound
        Out of tune foghorn duet
                Hungry donkey song

Catch it if you can
        The kiss 'twixt dusk and twilight
                As they bid goodnight

What to reveal when
        Take it slow or all at once
                Spring bud dilemma

ReBalancing

They navigate flows
Leaning on lampposts of hope
Outstanding approach

Clock change subterfuge
Pretend it hasn't happened
'til mid afternoon

Where sorrow and pain
Feel glimpses of sweet release
Then rainbows are made

ReBalancing

Such writing confines
Reading in between the lines
Sets the silenced free

Soft footed creatures
Traipse stardust over rooftops
During our slumbers

I choose not to fit
If I'm part of this puzzle
A big picture peace

ReBalancing

Some nifty advice
    Running in ill fitting shoes
        Could give you blisters

Unfulfilled demands
    Petulant peony blooms
        Staging a no show

Composing myself
    Like a comforting letter
        Or a calming song

ReBalancing

Paddling in oceans
Of cornflower dragonflies
Hope between their toes

Tug boat existence
Enabling grand adventures
Contented at port

Snack attack victim
Denuded of greenery
Leaf bone filigree

ReBalancing

By birds bees leaves trees
Mirrors and maybe ourselves
We've all been noticed

Even when we roam
Desperately far from home
Our essence remains

Memories and dreams
Nestled in the cracks between
The gift of presence

ReBalancing

Collect the anger
  Simmering throughout our world
  Fill the ozone hole

My philosophy
  Is positive realism
    Schrodinger's cat lived

Stripping off layers
  Mummified by others' needs
  Sure I'm underneath

ReBalancing

Spider uncertain
  Practising new web designs
   Is the world ready

Fights that can't be won
  People who undermine us
   Be brave walk away

Raucous lawnmowers
  Chainsaw off key symphonies
   Hoodlums of discord

ReBalancing

Clouds paper the sky
    Crashing seas craft salty mists
      The taste is of spring

I forgave at last
    Things they'd long since forgotten
      My burden to shed

Pace yourself they say
    To avoid the boom and bust
      How I'd love to boom

ReBalancing

All those bad reviews
  We wallpaper our heads with
    Need not be believed

Ladybird sunbathes
  Brain not lazy still spotting
    Opportunities

Sage for good advice
  Rosemary to remember
    Thyme's taste lingering

ReBalancing

Unexpected warmth
>   *Naked trees flex their bare bones*
>   *Readying for spring*

In soft winter nights
>   *Under magical moonlight*
>   *Angels build snowmen*

Borrow them awhile
>   *The best version of yourself*
>   *Live life through their eyes*

ReBalancing

Freeing thoughts and fears
Letting them land where they will
I'm testifying

Effortless supreme
Pair of red kite birds of prey
Spiralling from view

Statue sweating heat
Sweltering melting city
Fat raindrop respite

ReBalancing

Precision saunter
  Somewhere between a dawdle
    And a meander

Transient canvas
  Charcoal drifts smudge out the moon
    Nature the artist

Crumpled end of day
  Tattered with grubby edges
    Tomorrow renews

ReBalancing

Bubble enchantment
  Firm belief in unicorns
    Remnants of childhood

Fence hedge pavement wall
  Physical emotional
    Respect boundary

If winter has won
  Summer has summed spring has sprung
    What has autumn done

ReBalancing

Coconut shell home
   We carry and hide in it
      Me and my eight legs

Tasting ideas
   Which are the ones that tingle
      Running from the script

Shivers of self doubt
   Warm them with love and kindness
      We're works in progress

ReBalancing

Foibles a-plenty
Eccentricity a plus
Humans trump robots

Hastily scrawled trees
Sole grey on grey focal points
Stark moving skyscape

Steamed up shop windows
Muted lights gleam between us
Damp November towns

ReBalancing

Life happens right now
  Not then or when if or but
    They're all in our minds

The hush before dusk
  Birds soundlessly rehearsing
    Before bursting forth

Spring cleaning our minds
  Be more who we want to be
    Let your you shine through

ReBalancing

Truth can be a risk
To find see believe reveal
Your choice with your truth

You we they any
I'm the only me I have
Each one of us counts

All becomes muted
Colours sounds movements and thought
Harsh edges removed

ReBalancing

Wrapped up in a bow
Sometimes I'd like life to be
Neat simple sorted

I won one thing once
Heading for the furthest first
Best potato race

Torn paper thin skin
One touch bruises them purple
Unbreakable love

ReBalancing

Dawn lawn wrapped in frost
        Twinkling sheen on car windscreens
                Winter has landed

Swerving around fear
        Briefly waiting at patience
                Parks safely at peace

I have drowning days
        Calmly treading water days
                Randomly I soar

ReBalancing

Raspberry Sundays
Lazy endless afternoons
School homework is done

In our family
We're carrying the same genes
Different baggage

Life interrupted
Illness sorrow grief loss pain
Tempos ebb and flow

ReBalancing

Words are powerful
> *Those said to others and those*
> *We say to ourselves*

Kitchen shelves adorned
> *Sunbeams captured forever*
> *Smiles that never fade*

Tempted not to watch
> *Bubbles play knowing their fate*
> *Mistaken logic*

ReBalancing

Rarely visible
  Constellations of heartbeats
    Comforting our souls

Early morn rooftop
  Birds stomping in hobnail boots
    Trespass in my sleep

Was I a dragon
  I remember flying but
    Details elude me

ReBalancing

What right does right brain
       Have to have left left brain and
               Right brain think it's right

I've felt powerless
       Anxious dispirited low
               Writing rescues me

Beholden to none
       Not queen nor king nor empire
               Merely my own state

ReBalancing

Scalding black coffee
Or mellow camomile tea
Mood barometer

Tears of self pity
Validating corrosive
Cried out I look up

I locked all the doors
A maze of my own making
Courage is the key

ReBalancing

Open star clusters
Gravity binds as they drift
Cosmic roots and wings

Water boatmen bugs
Swim skim and carry bubbles
Bonus of both worlds

Swaddled in daydreams
Sudden Earth shattering bang
Time hiccups awake

ReBalancing

Removing cocoons
Exposes fragility
Dizzying freedoms

Breezing through the room
Bringer of kindness and cheer
Much of it lingers

Useful pause button
Fast forward and rewind can
Leave no room for now

ReBalancing

Love is the driver
  Of humanity's heartbeat
    Compassion its strength

Treasured belovéd
  Priceless shells studding the sand
    Mermaid offerings

Mischievous twinkle
  Slips into sight when they smile
    Decades slide away

ReBalancing

Dodging daily news
Avoiding gritty dramas
Helps my keel even

Picture a snow globe
Honouring your best moments
Describe it for me

Rain spills from the clouds
As if running for shelter
Parched landscapes oblige

ReBalancing

Once upon a dream
    Swept up on butterfly breath
        Nestled in star trails

Unsure what to do
    How to move how to manage
        I think of your smile

Swaying with currents
    Gilded with fragility
        Gracefully assured

ReBalancing

Football time travel
Running and passing the ball
To their future selves

Highly specialised
Allows me to live on Earth
I'm not my body

Brisk compact actions
Nothing expansive ornate
Woodpecker wisdom

ReBalancing

Cherry blossom morn
Strung with opportunities
There for the making

Negative comments
Linger long in my psyche
Praise is fleet of foot

Stray spirits wander
In worlds of mists where love sits
And eagles ponder

ReBalancing

Scurrying around
Researching time saving tips
I'm pleading guilty

Home made construction
Sturdy of opinion yet
Defenceless to joy

Scoured on mountain sides
Lilted by millions of wings
Notes from the ancients

ReBalancing

Emperor's new clothes
Like them does no one mention
Saturn's halo's slipped

Floundering inside
Searching for a firm footing
Side effect of life

Icicle clad heart
Carefully climate controlled
Thaws as snowflakes fall

ReBalancing

Grandpa reminds us
    Words don't need polish or shine
      Truth kind of glistens

No need to give up
    We live on a planet with
      Endless horizons

Dirty clean unseen
    Frail massive young dainty strong
      Hands that have helped me

ReBalancing

Rose bows to winter
   Clings to dreams of meeting the
      Majesty of spring

Agéd sun dozes
   Flashback to days long gone by
      When dinosaurs roamed

Floods of random thoughts
   Fished out dried off examined
      Those shared will flourish

ReBalancing

Cool blue white icebergs
  Protect pops of purest air
    Which gurgle and sing

Before approaching
  We advise listening to
    The sound of their face

Brash city skyline
  Parading opulent wares
    Softens as day breaks

ReBalancing

Full of potential
*   Each second a brand new start*
*   Sixty a minute*

Every one of us
*   Can harmonise with the world*
*   Music doesn't judge*

Murky moody sea
*   Threshing its way to the shore*
*   Grumbling in the depths*

ReBalancing

Neglect and abuse
    Gods review our custody
      Of the planet Earth

Upon first waking
    Disconnect 'twixt dream and fact
      Slumber wonderland

As we lonelys do
    I often talk to myself
      Silencing silence

ReBalancing

Holiday reading
Emblazoned across our chests
Tight T-shirt wisdom

Artful recycling
Laughter captured by the frost
Eco graffiti

Our pre assigned roles
Ripe for subtle subversion
We could improvise

ReBalancing

Rivers of regret
  Cascading back to the past
    Forgiveness quells them

Homes woven with care
  Dandelion charm carpets
    Ceilings optional

Smiles of sweet birdsong
  Scent of sunshine on the breeze
    Tenderness of dusk

ReBalancing

Poetry listens
    Responding to emotions
        Interpretively

Feeling under siege
    Decisions crowding around
        Pause ponder begin

Beneath the façade
    Of slightly fading glory
        Steely foundations

ReBalancing

Joyful or afraid
    They reach for each other's eyes
    Silent eloquence

Starstuff we're made of
    Once graced magnificent skies
    All life is revered

Shades of day mingle
    Saying hellos and goodbyes
    Honeyed horizon

ReBalancing

Polarisation
> *Somewhere between the extremes*
> > *A milder climate*

Slow to awaken
> *Insist on conversations*
> > *Technology woes*

Fragments of their life
> *Hide behind the looking glass*
> > *They shied away from*

ReBalancing

Turmoil confusion
My mind a word tornado
Please line up in rows

The heavens have burst
Crying so hard that it hurts
Profoundly relieved

They lived like pencils
Afraid erasers to hand
Now they paint neon

ReBalancing

Belting out show tunes
With gusto inside their head
We follow our bliss

Immersed in great books
I read more and more slowly
Reluctant to leave

Love loss and longing
Impermanent beach tattoos
Still leaving our marks

ReBalancing

Too many false starts
    Running someone else's race
    Our route at our pace

Mischievous sunbeams
    Silently sneak round curtains
    Bidding rise and shine

Soft thud from above
    Elves from shelves abscond at night
    Grudge match snowball fight

ReBalancing

Lackadaisical
A lazy eye for detail
Skilled at finding peace

Sticks stones and names hurt
I'm thinking of inventing
Teflon coated skin

Doldrums on offer
With optional wallowing
Tempting but declined

ReBalancing

My guilty treasures
These resentments and grudges
Are not worth the cost

Indignant tulip
Furious at being picked
Archly hangs its head

Tolerance no smile
Acceptance maybe a smile
Welcome open arms

ReBalancing

All their detailed plans
　　　　Tilt towards glowing futures
　　　　　　Where did today go

Blank page a clear stage
　　　　Inhabit it as you will
　　　　　　A tone steps words thought

We are not for sale
　　　　Each one of us is unique
　　　　　　Why try to label

ReBalancing

How do we best choose
What to fight for when to quit
Instinct or logic

Duvet immersion
Savouring the dregs of sleep
Readying for wake

Turbulent waters
Keeping them outside ourselves
Helps keep us afloat

ReBalancing

Hollowness inside
    Sorrow echoes round their soul
      Yearning for release

In threatening skies
    Butterflies still flutter by
      Dragonflies still roar

Trivial question
    Ferreting around my head
      Exhaustive research

ReBalancing

Nature reminds us
Perfect is overrated
Look at the Moon's scars

Body language speaks
To inner and outer worlds
Disguise optional

Tarnished over years
Things I thought I'd do or be
Polish or rethink

ReBalancing

Creepy creaks and groans
Alone in the house at night
Maybe it's dancing

Your secret scarred me
I threw it down waterfalls
Wounds are now healing

Skimming iced mountains
Inky velvet blue ceiling
Strung with faerie lights

ReBalancing

Body less nimble
> *Mind travels 'twixt now and then*
> *Spirit undaunted*

Orange blossom dreams
> *Brimming possibilities*
> *The flavours of spring*

Hearts beat in rhythm
> *Through all known and unknown worlds*
> *Primal connection*

ReBalancing

Error of judgement
　　No intricate craftsmanship
　　　Mistakes lack intent

All around their home
　　To guide when lost and alone
　　　Glow in the dark stars

Journey's milestone passed
　　First rush of independence
　　　Stabilisers gone

ReBalancing

Quicksand of worry
Artful diversions calling
New neural pathways

Tastefully discreet
Keeping everything treasured
In one simple heart

Ducking and diving
Living surviving striving
Life is for thriving

ReBalancing

I feel I'm obscured
    By all their preconceptions
        One day they'll see me

We by taking charge
    Positive or negative
        Choose our own orbit

In spite of setbacks
    Relentless slew of bad news
        Hope is defiant

ReBalancing

Fun flies waiting grates
Time moves at different speeds
Last Tuesday escaped

Smile into mirrors
Look deep into your own eyes
Fully accept you

Oh so bold robin
Bored of posing for Christmas
Dives in for the feast

ReBalancing

Every time we weep
  The Earth shifts on its axis
    Ever so slightly

Listening's a skill
  Hardest words to interpret
    Are the silent ones

Thoughts tumbling stumbling
  Sliding just out of reach or
    Playing hide and seek

ReBalancing

Hedgerow foraging
Faces and fingers purple
Blackberry August

Climbing those ladders
Watch out for slippery snakes
Risk of playing games

Life bewilders me
So much left to understand
Maybe that's its charm

ReBalancing

Their past our future
History plants DNA
Old stories reshaped

Those awaiting dawn
From seemingly endless night
A candle flickers

Having wasted years
Shrinking to fit their own lives
They unfold their wings

ReBalancing

Crystal reflections
    Offering fresh perspectives
      Everywhere we turn

Wrongly imprinted
    When those who should love us don't
      We're all lovable

Childhood friend shorthand
    Shared triumphs dreams and sorrows
      No need to explain

ReBalancing

Be your own critic
        Work out what to do better
                Forgive then progress

More sun fewer gusts
        Don't make trees moult all at once
                Autumn imploring

Craggy mood right now
        Hard edges and sharp splinters
                Songs from my teens soothe

ReBalancing

Toxic atmosphere
Smoke from other people's fires
More scenic routes sought

Birds swollen with song
Perched on roof top aerials
Proclaiming Earth's joys

My childhood taught me
To escape into stories
Heard read or made up

ReBalancing

Rain's playing a game
Reclaiming paths and pavements
Leaves giggle down drains

Cliffside greenery
Leaning precariously
Steep deep-rooted trust

March's icy blasts
Stride across huddled hilltops
Carousing with clouds

ReBalancing

Two elderly gents
 Doffing their caps in farewell
  Heartfelt courtesy

When life's going well
 Tinkering with the magic
  Risks breaking the spell

Quivers of hedgehogs
 Snuffle into back gardens
  After midnight feasts

ReBalancing

We need reminding
    As lonely we are waiting
        Ice melts and snow thaws

Tightly wound worries
    Pick one strand gently unwind
        Show it light love hope

Blank featureless sky
    Imagination crayons
        Abstract masterpiece

ReBalancing

As I get older
Learning to see through the rain
Joy between the drops

Messy address book
Folk who have moved or moved on
Bittersweet journeys

Rainy day faeries
Go fishing in wishing wells
Caught wishes come true

ReBalancing

Chosen spokespeople
    For all damaged selves beseech
      Be kind to your self

Humble apple core
    Once discarded but guarding
      Seeds from which trees grow

Old chained treasure chest
    Fear protected my heart with
      I'm picking the lock

ReBalancing

Sluggish Sunday morn
  Dawn tiptoes over the land
    Begging birds to shush

I'm holding no trumps
  No picture cards no aces
    Proudly plainly me

Over many years
  They've faithfully paid their dues
    Where is their receipt

ReBalancing

Free to take note of
People's pronouncements on us
More freeing not to

Dash straight out of bed
Or just one limb at a time
Cold room quandary

Dark of night barter
Mind switch off listen later
Sleep's the stuff of dreams

ReBalancing

All of creation
    Sings a song of gratitude
      Another sun rise

Wings newly unfurled
    Stunned by their magnificence
      They prepare to fly

Totally smitten
    February is pleading
      For one extra date

ReBalancing

Whilst all efforts have been taken to check, if there are words that appear to have too many or too few syllables for a haiku to adhere to the 5,7,5 rule, perhaps the reader could be kind enough to think of these as poetic emphasis? All perceived mistakes are, of course, my own.

ReBalancing

ReBalancing is available on Amazon in both Kindle and paperback versions.

Also by Charley Elbow

Small Feats and Tall Tales a book of poetry, haiku and 12 word stories for children.

"a lovely collection of poems" Give a Book charity

Available in Kindle and paperback from Amazon.

Together We'll See a painting and poetry book for all ages, in collaboration with artist John Pelham.

Available in paperback from Amazon.

Making A Scene combines Charley's poetry with the black and white photography of Steve Ward.
Available in Kindle and paperback from Amazon.

ReBalancing

Thanks go to Rachel who planted the seed from which this book grew. Your input, enthusiasm and support are invaluable.

Thanks, as ever, to Steve Ward for the beautiful cover photo, design and interior layout.

Steve is also the publisher and provides all the techie stuff necessary to get a book to print in paperback and Kindle.

Printed in Great Britain
by Amazon